JEZEBEL AND PROPHETIC MINISTRY

by Jonas Clark

JEZEBEL AND PROPHETIC MINISTRY

ISBN-10: 1-886885-30-3
ISBN-13: 978-1-886885-30-1

Published by Spirit of Life Publishing
27 West Hallandale Beach Blvd.
Hallandale, Florida, 33009-5437, U.S.A.
(954) 456-4420
www.JonasClark.com

JEZEBEL AND PROPHETIC MINISTRY

Following Jezebel's prophets can get you killed. Jezebel is a prophetess and teacher, cunning, deceptive, controlling and the number one adversary of Christ' five-fold ascension gift prophets.

Jezebel was the daughter of Ethbal, king of the Sidonians. Her father was the high priest of the goddess Ashtoreth a female deity. She was given to wed Ahab king of Israel to form a covenant between the two nations. Jezebel was a wicked queen. She set out to murder the prophets of Jehovah by the thousands. The few that remained hid themselves in caves. Others compromised their prophetic ministries and gave themselves to her.

JEZEBEL'S PROPHETIC MINISTRY

Jezebel was a prophetess. She served a foreign spirit named Ashtoreth. One of her noted traits was her ability to teach and train people for prophetic ministry. She has a large following today. Every generation must guard themselves from this seducing goddess of war that will hijack the prophetic ministry in every generation when given the chance. Jezebel is a false prophetess and teacher, cunning, deceptive, controlling and

*Know the logos,
judge everything you hear,
examine the fruit every prophet's life
and pray for the Holy Spirit's
discernment. Avoid her and
her prophetic network at all cost.*

the number one adversary of Christ's five-fold ascension gift prophets.

Every prophet should be thoroughly schooled in recognizing Jezebel's ministry. Her servants look to her leadership. She can preach, pray and prophesy better than anyone you have ever encountered. She is crafty, cunning, alluring and deceptive. Know the logos, judge everything you hear, examine the fruit

Prophets should always have permission, unction, before they prophesy.

of every prophet's life and pray for the Holy Spirit's discernment. Avoid her and her prophetic network at all cost. She is deadly and thousands have been slain by her. Could you be next? She is watching you right now.

Following the prophets of Jezebel can get you killed. That's what happened to Ahab. Let's read his story. Syria and Israel were at peace with each other but King Ahab wanted to expand his kingdom. He sought a confederacy with King Jehoshaphat of Judah to aid him in the invasion. Ahab told Jehoshaphat, "Everything the king of Syria has is ours for the taking." Jehoshaphat was not convinced.

He wanted a confirmation from Jehovah.

> "Then the king of Israel gathered the
> prophets together, about four hundred
> men, and said to them, 'Shall I go against
> Ramothgilead to battle or shall I forbear?'
> And they said, 'Go up for the Lord shall
> deliver it into the hand of the king.'" (1
> Kings 22:5-6)

You have already learned that prophets should
always have permission, unction, before they
prophesy. If they don't and someone approaches
them for a prophetic Word, God said,

> "I the Lord will answer them that cometh
> according to the multitude of his idols"
> (Ezekiel 4:4).

In other words, "I will tell him what he wants to hear." Ahab is an example of such a person with idolatry in his heart. The prophets of Jezebel responded to the king's inquiry. "Go up and conquer for the Lord will deliver it into the hand of the king." Four hundred prophets speaking the same thing, can you imagine that?

> "And Jehoshaphat said, 'Is there not here a prophet of the Lord besides these that we might inquire of him?'" (1 Kings 22:7)

Jehoshaphat sensed that something was not right with these prophets and he asked for yet another.

> "And the king of Israel said to Jehoshaphat, 'There is yet one man, Micaiah the son of Imlah, by whom we may inquire of

the Lord: but I hate him; for he doth not prophesy good about me, but evil.' And Jehoshaphat said, 'Let not the king say so.'" (1 Kings 22:8)

Ahab said there was one other prophet they could ask. His name was Micaiah but Ahab hated him. King Ahab didn't like him because he never prophesied anything good. He much preferred the agreeable smooth sayings from Jezebel's prophets. Micaiah was the unliked prophet. Ahab was familiar with Jehovah's prophets. He had been troubled by another named Elijah that prophesied a 3-1/2 year drought (1 Kings 17).

"Then the king of Israel called an officer and said, 'Hasten hither Micaiah the son

They prophesied smooth sayings of victory from the spirit of divination and witchcraft.

of Imlah.' And the king of Israel and Jehoshaphat the king of Judah sat each on his throne, having put on their robes in a void place in the entrance of the gate of Samaria and all the prophets prophesied before them." (1 Kings 22:9-10)

King Ahab sent for Micaiah. While the two kings waited at the city gate four hundred prophets of Jezebel prophesied one after the other what Ahab wanted to hear. They prophesied smooth sayings of victory from the spirit of divination and witchcraft. You may find yourself in large meetings with hundreds of prophets prophesying the same thing. If so look to the Holy Spirit and an inner-witness before agreeing. Most importantly confirm everything said with the Word of God.

> "And Zedekiah the son of Chenaanah made him horns of iron and he said, 'Thus saith the Lord with these shalt thou push the Syrians until thou have consumed them.'" (1 Kings 22:11)

Among this prophetic gathering rose a bold prophet named Zedekiah. He got everybody's attention as he stepped forward and said, "Thus saith the Lord!" He grasped the iron horns firmly in his aged hands as prophetic symbols. "With these you shall push the Syrians until they are destroyed," he said.

*Unlike the prophet Balaam who
fell because he wanted the "rewards
of divination," Micaiah was not
persuaded by anyone but Jehovah.
Being popular among other prophets
was not in his heart.*

Everybody listened intently including the other
three hundred ninety-nine prophets and both kings.
It seemed like Zedekiah was speaking as one with
authority.

> "And all the prophets prophesied so,
> saying, 'Go up to Ramothgilead and
> prosper for the Lord shall deliver it into
> the king's hand.'" (1 Kings 22:12)

Everyone heard the elder Zedekiah prophesy. All the prophets were in agreement. Public opinion was set. There was only one other prophet to hear, Micaiah.

> "And the messenger that was gone to call Micaiah spake to him, saying, 'Behold now the words of the prophets declare good to the king with one mouth: let thy word, I pray thee, be like the word of one of them and speak that which is good.'"
> (1 Kings 22:13)

King Ahab sent for Micaiah. After finding him, his escort told him what was going on and the good prophecies of the other prophets.

"And Micaiah said, 'As the Lord liveth, what the Lord saith to me, that will I speak.'" (1 Kings 22:14)

AHAB'S DECEPTION

Let's make sure we understand what Micaiah, God's prophet said. "As the Lord lives I will speak what the Lord says." God is about to use Micaiah to answer Ahab's inquiry "according to the idolatry in his heart." He is going to tell him what he wants to hear. Are you ready for this?

"So he came to the king. And the king said to him, 'Micaiah, shall we go against Ramothgilead to battle or shall we forbear?' And he answered him, 'Go and

prosper for the Lord shall deliver it into
the hand of the king.'" (1 Kings 22:15)

Now, if you are confused, read closely. What in
the world is going on? What was it that Micaiah said?
He said, "Whatever the Lord says that will I speak."
Now what was it the Lord spoke through Micaiah?
"Go and prosper for the Lord shall deliver it into the
hand of the king." Again we see God answer someone
according to the idolatry in their heart. King Ahab
put "the stumbling block of his iniquity" before
the prophet (Ezekiel 14:3) and Micaiah prophesied
the same smooth saying as the other four hundred
prophets. Amazing!

"And the king said to him, 'How many
times shall I adjure thee that thou tell me

nothing but that which is true in the name
of the Lord?" (1 Kings 22:16)

Micaiah had always prophesied contrary things
to King Ahab. Ahab doesn't believe his own ears.
Even Ahab was wise enough to know that something
was not right. Micaiah then spoke the true "Word of
the Lord." Watch this.

"And he said, 'I saw all Israel scattered on
the hills as sheep that have not a shepherd
and the Lord said these have no master,
let them return every man to his house in
peace.'" (1 Kings 22:17)

Does this prophetic utterance say that all will go
well with the kings? No! Let's continue.

"And the king of Israel said to Jehoshaphat, "Did I not tell thee that he would prophesy no good about me, but evil?" And he said, "Hear thou therefore the word of the Lord: I saw the Lord sitting on his throne and all the host of heaven standing by him on his right hand and on his left." (1 Kings 22:18-19)

Unlike the prophet Balaam who fell because he wanted the "rewards of divination," Micaiah was not persuaded by anyone but Jehovah. Being popular among other prophets was not in his heart. Here we see a true prophet's heart. All prophets must guard their hearts from the lure of public admiration. King Ahab had idolatry in his heart. He wanted to conquer Syria and would do it at all cost.

JEZEBEL AND LYING SPIRITS

Micaiah first answered Ahab according to his idolatry but by God's mercy released a true prophetic utterance. Would Ahab have ears to hear? Or was his idolatry and covetousness going to lead him into error? Let's take a look behind the scenes at this prophetic gathering with the two kings. God drew back heaven's curtain to let us listen in on a conversation between Him and a lying spirit that would be allowed to deceive Jezebel's prophets.

> "And the Lord said, 'Who shall persuade Ahab that he may go up and fall at Ramothgilead?' And one said on this manner and another said on that manner. And there came forth a spirit and stood before the Lord and said, 'I will

persuade him.' And the Lord said to him, 'Wherewith?' And he said, 'I will go forth and I will be a lying spirit in the mouth of all his prophets.' And he said, 'Thou shalt persuade him and prevail also: go forth and do so" (1 Kings 22:20-22).

This Scripture teaches that God allowed a lying spirit to speak through these prophets because of King Ahab's idolatrous heart.

"Now therefore, behold, the Lord hath put a lying spirit in the mouth of all these thy prophets and the Lord hath spoken evil concerning thee. But Zedekiah the son of Chenaanah went near and smote Micaiah on the cheek and said, 'Which way went

Self-will, pride, idolatry and covetousness were the sins of Ahab. Following Jezebel's prophets can get you killed.

the spirit of the Lord from me to speak to thee?"(1 Kings 22:23-24)

FOLLOWING JEZEBEL

Zedekiah slapped Micaiah and asked, "How is it possible the Holy Spirit stopped using me and began to use you?" Prophetic error releases a spirit of pride. Zedekiah thought that he had put the amen on the prophetic conference. How dare Micaiah do something contrary! You may never be physically assaulted but you will be verbally attacked. Zedekiah was a well respected leader within that group. His physical assault proves that his heart wasn't right.

If something like this ever happens to you guard your heart and don't respond out of the flesh. It's best to say nothing and leave. Pull yourself together and pray. Then see what God says. Always take the high road. You are not one of Jezebel's prophets but a representative of Christ.

Ahab ignored the prophecy of Micaiah and followed the prophets of Jezebel. His army was defeated and he lost his life (1 Kings 22:37). Self-will, pride, idolatry and covetousness were the sins of Ahab. Following Jezebel's prophets can get you killed.

MEDITATION AND REFLECTION

Jezebel is a false prophetess and teacher, cunning, deceptive, controlling and the number one adversary of Christ's five-fold ascension gift prophets.

Every prophet should be thoroughly schooled in recognizing Jezebel's ministry.

Following the prophecies of Jezebel can get you killed.

Micaiah was the unliked prophet.

King Ahab put "the stumbling block of his iniquity" before the prophet (Ezekiel 14:3) and Micaiah prophesied the same smooth saying as the other four hundred prophets.

Unlike the prophet Balaam who fell because he wanted the "rewards of divination," Micaiah was not persuaded by anyone but Jehovah.

All prophets must guard their hearts from the lure of public admiration.

Micaiah first answered Ahab according to his idolatry but by God's mercy released a true prophetic utterance.

God drew back heaven's curtain to let us listen in on a conversation between Him and a lying spirit that would be allowed to deceive Jezebel's prophets.

Prophetic error releases a spirit of pride.

Ahab ignored the prophecy of Micaiah and followed the prophets of Jezebel. His army was defeated and he lost his life (1 Kings 22:37).

Self-will, pride, idolatry and covetousness were the sins of Ahab.

Following Jezebel's prophets can get you killed.

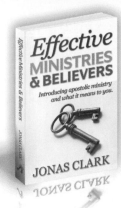

EFFECTIVE MINISTRIES & BELIEVERS:
INTRODUCING APOSTOLIC MINISTRY AND WHAT IT MEANS TO YOU

ISBN 1-886885-25-7

Christ's disciples have fought raging spiritual battles with Satan for centuries. Some failed, others experienced limited success, but there is another group, effective believers that discovered the secret to victorious living. This group was taught by apostles that Christ would "build His Church and the gates of hell would not prevail against it."

Those who want to do great exploits for Christ need to read this book.

Discover your authority:
• How the apostles taught believers to turn the world upside down.
• How apostolic design empowers every believer for breakthrough.
• How to become a spiritual warrior, reformer and prophetic strategists.
• How apostolic restoration and reformation principles advance your calling.

To order, log on to www.JonasClark.com or call 800.943.6490.

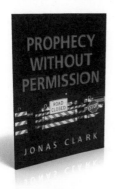

Equipping Resources by Jonas Clark

Pocket-Size Books

Entering Prophetic Ministry

Prophecy Without Permission

How Witchcraft Spirits Attack

Seeing What Others Can't

Unlocking Prophetic Imaginations

Books

Extreme Prophetic Studies

Advanced Apostolic Studies

Kingdom Living: How to Activate Your Spiritual Authority

Imaginations: Dare to Win the Battle Against Your Mind

Jezebel, Seducing Goddess of War *(Also Available in Spanish)*

Exposing Spiritual Witchraft

30 Pieces of Silver *(Overcoming Religious Spirits)*

The Apostolic Equipping Dimension

Effective Ministries & Believers

Life After Rejection: God's Path to Emotional Healing

Come Out! A Handbook for the Serious Deliverance Minister

www.JonasClark.com